Best Practices for Teaching

MATHEMATICS

D1565760

Other Corwin Press Books by Randi Stone

Best Practices for Teaching Science: What Award-Winning Classroom Teachers Do, 2007

Best Practices for Teaching Writing: What Award-Winning Classroom Teachers Do, 2007

Best Classroom Management Practices for Reaching All Learners: What Award-Winning Classroom Teachers Do, 2005

Best Teaching Practices for Reaching All Learners: What Award-Winning Classroom Teachers Do, 2004

What?! Another New Mandate? What Award-Winning Teachers Do When School Rules Change, 2002

Best Practices for High School Classrooms: What Award-Winning Secondary Teachers Do, 2001

Best Classroom Practices: What Award-Winning Elementary Teachers Do, 1999

New Ways to Teach Using Cable Television: A Step-by-Step Guide, 1997

Best Practices for Teaching

MATHEMATICS

What Award-Winning Classroom Teachers Do

RANDI STONE

CORWIN PRESS
A SAGE Publications Company
Thousand Oaks, CA 91320

For information:

Corwin Press
A Sage Publications Company
2455 Teller Road
Thousand Oaks, California 91320
www.corwinpress.com

Sage Publications Ltd.
1 Oliver's Yard
55 City Road
London EC1Y 1SP
United Kingdom

Sage Publications India Pvt. Ltd.
B 1/I 1 Mohan Cooperative
    Industrial Area
Mathura Road, New Delhi 110 044
India

Sage Publications Asia-Pacific Pte Ltd
33 Pekin Street #02-01
Far East Square
Singapore 048763

Printed in the United States of America

Library of Congress Cataloging-in-Publication Data

Stone, Randi.
Best practices for teaching mathematics: What award-winning classroom teachers do / Randi Stone.
    p. cm.
Includes index.
ISBN 978-1-4129-2454-2 (cloth) — ISBN 978-1-4129-2455-9 (pbk.)
    1. Mathematics—Study and teaching (Elementary)—United States—Case studies.
2. Mathematics—Study and teaching (Secondary)—United States—Case studies.
3. Effective teaching—United States—Case studies. I. Title.
QA135.6.S76 2007
372.7'2—dc22

                                        2006034224

This book is printed on acid-free paper.

07   08   09   10   11   10   9   8   7   6   5   4   3   2   1

Acquisitions Editor:	Faye Zucker
Editorial Assistant:	Gem Rabanera
Production Editor:	Melanie Birdsall
Typesetter:	C&M Digitals (P) Ltd.
Copy Editor:	Bill Bowers
Proofreader:	Cheryl Rivard
Indexer:	Michael Ferreira
Cover Designer:	Scott Van Atta

Contents

Preface

In the pages that follow, award-winning teachers generously share their best teaching practices with us. I hope you enjoy reading about their classrooms and trying out their teaching techniques as much as I have. This group of teachers has more than 400 years of combined teaching experience.

Acknowledgments

Thank you to a wonderful group of teachers for sharing your stories with us.

About the Author

 **Randi Stone** is a graduate of Clark University, Boston University, and Salem State College. She completed her doctorate in education at the University of Massachusetts, Lowell. She is the author of nine Corwin Press books, including her latest in a series: *Best Practices for Teaching Writing: What Award-Winning Classroom Teachers Do, Best Practices for Teaching Mathematics: What Award-Winning Classroom Teachers Do,* and *Best Practices for Teaching Science: What Award-Winning Classroom Teachers Do.* She lives with her teenage daughter, Blair, in Keene, New Hampshire.

About the Contributors

Carol Ann Amos, Teacher Leader/Mathematics Coordinator
Twinfield Union
106 Nasmith Brook Road
Plainfield, Vermont 05667
School Telephone Number: (802) 426-3213, ext. 242
E-mail: camossut@yahoo.com

Number of Years Teaching: 20
Awards: Presidential Award for Excellence in Mathematics and
Science Teaching (PAEMST), 2004

Sharon Andrews, Fifth-Grade Teacher
Challenge Center at Mark Twain Elementary
315 West 27th Street
Sioux Falls, South Dakota 57108
School Telephone Number: (605) 367-4560
E-mail: andresha@sf.k12.sd.us

Number of Years Teaching: 13
Awards: Presidential Award for Excellence in Mathematics and
Science Teaching (PAEMST), 2003
Huber Scholarship for Outstanding Doctoral
Student in Curriculum and Instruction,
University of South Dakota, Vermillion, 1999

Terry Castoria, Mathematics Teacher
Marlboro Middle School
County Road 520
Marlboro, New Jersey 07746
School Telephone Number: (732) 972-2100
E-mail: tcastoria@marlboro.k12.nj.us

Number of Years Teaching: 10
Awards: Disney Teacher Award, 2006
             Edyth May Sliffe Award, Distinguished Mathematics
             Teaching, 2005

Patricia F. Clark, First-Grade Teacher
Gotham Avenue School
181 Gotham Avenue
Elmont, New York 11003
School Telephone Number: (516) 326-5540
E-mail: wesynch@optonline.net

Number of Years Teaching: 23
Awards: Who's Who in American Teachers, 2004–2005
             Scott Foresman National Teacher Award, 2000
             National Teachers Hall of Fame, 2000

Joyce Wolfe Dodd, Sixth-Grade Mathematics Teacher
Bryson Middle School
3657 S. Industrial Drive
Simpsonville, South Carolina 29681
School Telephone Number: (864) 355-2135
E-mail: jdodd@greenville.k12.sc.us

Number of Years Teaching: 34
Awards: Presidential Award for Excellence in Teaching
             Mathematics and Science (PAEMST), 2004
             State Finalist Award for Excellence in Teaching
             Mathematics and Science, 2004
             National Board Certification for Early
             Adolescence Mathematics, 2002

Ryan Faulk, Second-Grade Teacher
Chief Joseph Elementary
5305 3rd Ave. South
Great Falls, Montana 59405
School Telephone Number: (406) 268-6675
E-mail: ryan_faulk@gfps.k12.mt.us

Number of Years Teaching: 7
Awards: Phi Delta Kappa Wal-Mart Montana Teacher of
the Year, 2005

Debbie Gordon, Third-Grade Teacher
Madison Simis School
7302 No. 10th Street
Phoenix, Arizona 85020
School Telephone Number: (602) 664-7300
E-mail: dgordon@msd38.org

Number of Years Teaching: 19
Award: Presidential Award for Excellence in Mathematics and
Science Teaching (PAEMST), 2002

Donna H. Henry, Fourth-Grade Teacher
Shumway Elementary
1310 W. Palo Verde Drive
Chandler, Arizona 85224
School Telephone Number: (480) 812-7400
E-mail: dhhenry4@cox.net

Number of Years Teaching: 25
Award: Presidential Award for Excellence in Mathematics and
Science Teaching (PAEMST), 2004

Debra Rose Howell, NBCT (National Board Certified Teacher)
Multiage Teacher
Monte Cristo Elementary
1201 100th St. NE
Granite Falls, Washington 98252
School Telephone Number: (360) 691-7718
E-mail: debrarose8@aol.com

Number of Years Teaching: 22
Awards: Golden Apple Award, 2005
         Regional Teacher of the Year, Washington State, 2005
         Masonic Temple–Scottish Rite Teacher of the Year
           for Washington State, 2004

Helen F. Melvin, Second-Grade Teacher
Dr. Levesque School
443 U.S. Rte 1
P.O. Box 489
Fort Kent, Maine 04743
School Telephone Number: (207) 543-7302
E-mail: h_melvin@hotmail.com

Number of Years Teaching: 36
Awards: Fleet Grant Award, 2003
         National Semiconductor Internet Innovator Award, 2002
         Spreading Educator-to-Educator Developments
           (SEED) Award, 2002

Jim Miller, Math/Science Teacher
Cle Elum Roslyn High School
2692 SR 903
Cle Elum, Washington 98922
School Telephone Number: (509) 649-2291
E-mail: millerj@cleelum.wednet.edu

Number of Years Teaching: 30
Awards: Washington State Mathematics Council Educator
           of the Year, 2004
         Toyota Tapestry Grant
         Woodrow Wilson National Fellow, Math
           Traveling Team

Dianne M. Peterson, Fifth-Grade Teacher
Surfside Elementary
475 Cassia Blvd.
Satellite Beach, Florida 32937
School Telephone Number: (321) 773-2818
E-mail: petersond@brevard.k12.fl.us

Number of Years Teaching: 30
Awards: Presidential Award for Excellence in Mathematics and
            Science Teaching (PAEMST), 2004
            Presidential Award for Excellence in Mathematics and
            Science Teaching (PAEMST) Finalist, 2002

John P. Pieper, Fifth-Grade Teacher
Webster Stanley Elementary School
915 Hazel St.
Oshkosh, Wisconsin 54901
School Telephone Number: (920) 424-0460
E-mail: jpieper@new.rr.com

Number of Years Teaching: 25
Awards: Japan Fulbright Memorial Fund Scholar, 2005
            Disney Teacher Award, 2003

Pam Roller, Second-Grade Teacher
Galveston Elementary
401 South Maple Street
Galveston, Indiana 46932
School Telephone Number: (574) 699-6687
E-mail: rollerp@sesc.k12.in.us

Number of Years Teaching: 32
Awards: Japan Fulbright Memorial Fund Teacher
            Participant, 2005
            Disney Teacher Award, 2003

Mary Jane Short, Second-Grade Teacher
Long Neck Elementary
Indian River School District
26064 School Lane
Millsboro, Delaware 19966
School Telephone Number: (302) 945-6200
E-mail: mjshort@irsd.k12.de.us

Number of Years Teaching: 29
Award: Presidential Award for Excellence in Mathematics and
           Science Teaching (PAEMST), 2004

Heather Sullivan, Seventh-Grade Mathematics Teacher
 Albuquerque Academy
 6400 Wyoming Blvd., NE
 Albuquerque, New Mexico 87109
 School Telephone Number: (505) 828-3179
 E-mail: sullivan@aa.edu

 Number of Years Teaching: 5
 Award: Disney Teacher Award, 2005

Steven Wyborney, Fourth-/Fifth-Grade Looping Teacher
 Nyssa Elementary School
 809 Bower Avenue
 Nyssa, Oregon 97913
 School Telephone Number: (541) 372-3313
 E-mail: swyborney@nyssa.k12.or.us

 Number of Years Teaching: 11
 Awards: Oregon Teacher of the Year, 2005
     L.E. Wesche Outstanding Educator Award,
       Northwest Nazarene University, 2005
     Nyssa Chamber of Commerce Educator of
       the Year, 1998

To Blair, my darling daughter
To Bev, my dear friend

CHAPTER *1*

Using a Money-Based Discipline or Reward System in an Elementary Classroom

Ryan Faulk

Great Falls, Montana

O ne of the greatest challenges of educating children is helping them
make relevant connections to the world around them. Providing
a solid rationale is one of the foundations of an effective lesson, but a
rationale that seems perfectly reasonable to an adult may have little or
no impact on a child with minimal life experiences.

Even more challenging is trying to break through the indifferent attitudes of some students and get them to buy into a rationale for simply
being in school in the first place. I feel that a strong plan of discipline
and reward (one that inspires students and teaches core values) is the key.

I experimented with a number of different discipline/reward systems during my first few years of teaching. Some were certainly more effective than others, but none of them helped me to teach the students the importance of responsibility, respect, and effort, which are the core values I try to instill in each child. It was not until I began using money as the foundation of my discipline/reward system that I could see those values coming to fruition before my very eyes. I had previously seen money used sporadically in various classrooms at different grade levels. Most classrooms dabbled in the use of money and used a few pennies here and there as an occasional motivator.

If I were going to bring about academic and behavioral change in students, it would take a far greater commitment. I decided that a vibrant, realistic classroom economy was the key to encouraging what was most important to me as a teacher and what would be important to the students' success in my classroom. Little did I know that the extensive use of money in the classroom would be more successful than I had ever imagined.

The use of money is woven throughout virtually every aspect of the classroom and culminates with a "Friday Store" where students have the opportunity to spend their money and celebrate their accomplishments for the week. The students begin the week with a designated amount of classroom money that looks virtually identical to real money. Each week is a fresh start, so all students know that no matter how much they struggled the week prior, each student has a clean slate on Monday morning.

The money is kept in a tray in the student's desk. Keeping it handy allows the students to monitor their own progress throughout the week and to have instant access that does not disturb the rest of the class. The general philosophy is quite simple. Throughout the course of the week, students get money for the demonstration of responsibility, respect, and effort, and they lose it for failing to demonstrate those expectations.

For example, in my classroom, students get money for making quick and quiet transitions, returning homework daily, and showing kindness and respect to others. On the other hand, they get money taken away for failing to return homework (a rather large fine that forces compliance), interruptions, and not following directions. Whatever the teacher's goals are for a classroom, the money system can be adapted to meet his or her specific needs and classroom expectations.

Because my primary focus for the students is responsibility, I have placed a far greater monetary weight on the students being responsible. As a result, responsibility problems have virtually disappeared from my class. All assignments are turned in because both the penalty and the reward for responsibility are substantial.

There are probably 20 or so other little things I give money for throughout the course of a week, such as picking up messes, using good manners, or just simply demonstrating the kinds of deeds I want others to emulate. I tend to give a lot more than I take to reward and encourage students, but when I do take money, it is immediate and specific so the student understands his or her transgression. Over the course of a week, the amount of money the students have tends to fluctuate depending upon their behavior and responsibility.

The culmination of a week's worth of responsibility, respect, and effort is rewarded with the Friday Store. The Friday Store itself is an intricate but extremely powerful event to celebrate the demonstration of those traits that are important in both school and life. Prior to the store, there are a number of elements that must be in place.

First, all the student's class work and homework must be turned in. Any work not turned in is completed during the store visit. Next, each student completes a "summary" of their week on a form I hand out. They have to count how much they earned and decide if that was a good week or not.

They must also count how much money was saved from the prior week and add the two amounts together to see how much they can spend at the store. There is a space on the form where I can write a personal note to parents explaining their child's week. Prior to the store, I also give a bonus to those students who completed all homework assignments and fulfilled all their responsibilities throughout the week. I also award extra credit for work the students have completed at home or during center times. Finally, prior to the store, we do a math-related activity in which students can earn money for estimation.

Now on to the Friday Store! The store consists of a multitude of items donated from parents, businesses, colleagues, and, of course, my own pocketbook. There are snacks, drinks, toys, school supplies, activities, games, puzzles, and just about anything else a student of that age would like to purchase. The store is staffed with volunteer parents or older students in the upper grades. They perform the jobs of cashier and banker.

The cashier accepts the students' money and has the students figure the correct change before giving it to them. The banker is there so the students can either make change or trade their money in for different bills or coins. Initially the volunteers are involved in helping the students count the money and make decisions, but once the students begin to understand the concept of money, they are much more self-sufficient.

Purchasing from the store is not mandatory. The students are allowed to spend or save as much as they would like during the store. Money not spent at the store is kept in their "banks," which are simply pencil boxes with the students' names written on the outside. These banks are stored away for the following week in order to keep each week's earnings independent and easily scrutinized. The store itself takes only about twenty minutes, although setup and takedown require a little more time.

As with many things in life, the Friday Store is not a right—it's a privilege. Not all students are allowed to participate in the store on Friday. I establish a designated monetary amount the students must earn in order to participate, as well as a standard for responsibility and behavior. The students not participating are not ignored during this time, though.

I take advantage of the store time to conference with those students who did not meet the expectations for the week and thus were not allowed to participate in the store. This time is vital because it allows me to individually discuss the student's behavior and formulate a specific plan for achieving those goals in the upcoming week. For those students who were not allowed to participate in the store, I take time to write a specific message to parents detailing the problems their child had that week. I also require that the paper be signed by parents as both a consequence for the student as well as a means of record keeping and progress monitoring.

It would be impossible to explain all the intricacies of the money-based discipline/reward system because so much of it is very personal and specific to each classroom and each teacher. My description is merely a reflection of how I carry out a week and is by no means the only method of utilizing money in a classroom. Regardless of how a teacher implements and utilizes the system, there are details that take time to perfect over the course of each week as well as each school year. Different students have different needs, and each classroom has certain strengths and weaknesses that require a teacher to constantly monitor and adjust the money system accordingly.

The benefits of a money-based discipline system are greater than I had predicted. Parents rejoice over the dramatic improvement in their child's responsibility and effort. Other teachers praise the class's respect for rules and their display of good manners. I have personally noticed a drastic change in each child's intrinsic motivation for both learning and behavior. Children generally know right from wrong but often choose not to display the right behavior. The use of money has helped the students stop and consider their choices in a given situation because the consequences are more tangible.

Perhaps the greatest benefit has been the complete and total mastery of all benchmarks related to the understanding and use of money. By the end of the year, even my youngest second-grade students are proficient or advanced in counting money and making change. They are also beginning to understand the concepts of spending, saving, decision making, and other real-life uses of money.

The money-based discipline/reward system has worked exceptionally well in my classroom. I see the kinds of academic and behavioral benefits I strived for when all other discipline/reward plans failed. For those who are looking to maximize classroom management, increase student achievement, and teach students responsibility and respect, I would highly recommend using money in the classroom.

Helpful Tips

- The one area to be cautious about is rewarding money for academic reasons. The gain or loss of money does not make a child any smarter or more successful in a particular area. It can be very counterproductive if the lower-achieving students are not only struggling academically but also being left behind monetarily. Reward money for behavior, responsibility, and effort, which do promote self-esteem and further effort.

(Continued)

Helpful Tips (Continued)

- Volunteers are essential at the store to run the cashier and banker positions. They are also extremely helpful when it comes to setting up and putting away the store on Friday. The process can be quite time-consuming, and unless the teacher is blessed with a prep period or other extra time, Fridays can be rather hectic with no volunteers.
- Do not place restrictions on how much money the students can save and spend on a given Friday. Their spending habits are a reflection of real life, in which some people choose to spend and others choose to save. Every year there are kids who spend every cent every week. On the other hand, I once had a student who saved so much money that we brought in a live pet bird for her to purchase just so she would spend her money (with all the necessary permission, of course).

CHAPTER 2

Number of the Year Award

Terry Castoria

Marlboro, New Jersey

Congratulations! You have been selected to judge the Number of the Year Award contest sponsored by Ms. Castoria's math classes. The Number of the Year Award is given each year to the most important number in our number system. Our contestants, numbers 0 through 9, have been hard at work trying to persuade you to cast your vote for the number that you feel is most deserving of this prestigious award!

As you reflect on the qualifications of each contestant, consider their contributions to our society and the role each plays in our life. Think carefully about which number is truly the most important, which number we could not do without, which number has the greatest impact on our lives. Your decision should be based on *both* mathematical contributions made by this number as well as your personal experiences with this number.

After you have carefully made your selection, write a persuasive essay justifying your choice. Your essay should be a *minimum* of five paragraphs. Your first paragraph should begin with a thesis statement, including at least three reasons to support your choice for number of the year. The following three paragraphs should support each of the reasons listed in paragraph one. A concluding paragraph should summarize your position. Be as creative as you like!

Your essay should be typed, double-spaced. All work will be graded on both the math content and writing content. Remember, the lucky winner of our contest will be given an all-expenses-paid vacation to Integer Island! The final decision is up to you! Good luck and think carefully!

Decision due by _____

Helpful Tips

- This activity may be used at any time during the year. It is a great beginning-of-the-year activity, stimulating the creative juices after a long summer vacation! It can easily be used as a culminating activity for a persuasive writing unit integrating math with language arts, or as a final writing/math project to conclude the school year.
- The students are always eager to hear the final tabulated results. The number with the most essays is the winner! I create a bulletin board labeled with sections for each number, and the corresponding essays are hung below each number. The winning number has a cutout of a sunburst around it.
- A rubric is included. This rubric is predicated on the assumption that the math teacher will be grading the assignment. Should both the math teacher and the language arts teacher grade the essays separately, it would be better to use two separate rubrics, thereby isolating the math skills from the writing skills. Rubrics should be distributed at the time the activity is assigned, thus allowing the students to understand both what is expected of them and the grading criteria that will be used.

Some points to consider:

- Personal experiences with a number might be a particular number that seems to appear in a student's life frequently (all family members born in March, two people in the family, three pets, and so on).
- An unacceptable contribution by a number would be "the ability to count by" concept, since that could be applied to every number. (Many students have written that if we didn't have the chosen number in our lives, we couldn't count by it.)
- Students may decorate the margins of their essays, but I discourage a cover page or report cover.

Number of the Year Award Rubric

Score Point 4

- I have made a clear choice on this issue and I fully support it with three appropriate mathematical and personal references.
- I have demonstrated outstanding reasoning thoroughly connected to mathematical and personal references.
- I have demonstrated outstanding reasoning thoroughly connected to mathematical knowledge.
- I have an organization that is logical and that does not jump around.
- A forceful conclusion restates my choice.
- My work has no misspellings or grammatical errors and is neatly done.
- I understand the type of audience I am writing for and I use language and arguments that they will understand.

Score Point 3

- I have made a clear choice on this issue and I have somewhat supported it with three appropriate mathematical and personal references.
- I have demonstrated reasoning connected to mathematical knowledge.
- I have an organization that is logical but it strays a little.
- A conclusion restates my choice.
- My work has few misspellings or grammatical errors and is neatly done.
- I understand the type of audience I am writing for.

Score Point 2

- I have made a clear choice on this issue but I have minimal support using appropriate mathematical and personal references.
- I have demonstrated no reasoning connected to mathematical knowledge.
- I have no real organization.
- I do not have a conclusion.
- My work has many misspellings or grammatical errors and is not done neatly.
- I did not try to write for the audience.

CHAPTER 3

Technology-Enhanced Second-Grade Math

Helen F. Melvin

Fort Kent, Maine

What a difference technology has made in my second-grade classroom! Being a veteran teacher of 36 years, I remember teaching in the late 1960s with few materials other than textbooks, workbooks, chalkboard, and paper. Today I teach in a room filled with materials for hands-on instruction and I have my own classroom computer lab. I must say that the computers and technology materials in my room were acquired through educational grants.

Has technology changed my method of teaching math? You bet! One of the great benefits of having computers in a self-contained classroom is being able to individualize math instruction. The 18 computers in my classroom are networked and all have Internet access. I owe this techno-lab to the generosity and competence of my computer-literate brother, who designed and set up the network. The programs and makeup of the system were my experiment.

To meet the needs of all my students, I first had to compile first-, second-, and third-grade math skills. When the skills were identified, I searched the Internet for free math educational Web sites containing those skills and I saved the links. Using FrontPage, I created my own (in-class) Web site. All my classroom subjects are listed at the top of my opening Web page, and each is hyperlinked to its own subject page, where all the skills are linked to a Web site. These sites generally cater to various skill levels—this allows me to individualize and accommodate the needs of all students. Under the math hyperlink, I compiled a page of math skills (color-coded to differentiate the skills).

Examples of skills on the math link include addition and subtraction drills, clock drills, money, even and odd numbers, and counting by twos and threes, just to name a few. The sites selected are all free Internet educational Web sites, using enticing programming including games such as football, baseball, racing, *Jeopardy!,* and much more.

When students complete the assigned mandatory in-class math work, they are asked to go on the computer to continue working on math skills until the period ends. When on the computer, students are always assigned a specific math skill or a specific site to work on. The use of a previously researched Web site has been a tremendous asset to me in teaching. It has simplified planning for those who finish their work more quickly and places all my students' skills in full view when I open the math Web site. It is easy to assign challenging work for the more advanced students and to help students who need extra practice with specific skills. It has also cut back on some duplicating and correcting. The networking allows me to check on their progress at any time.

I have purchased ready-made math programs that allow the teacher to view the skills each student is working on and to check on his or her level of mastery. When purchasing programs, I always look for teacher/parent feedback features. Eventually I would like to use a math program that accelerates students automatically, as it monitors and tracks their mastery of skills. To date, such programs are expensive and beyond our school's financial means.

From the start of the school year, I discuss the use of computers in the classroom. Since these students are young, and at times test the system, any students who don't follow directions at the computer are told they will lose their computer privileges for the day and will need to complete their work at their desks.

Recently I had a second-grade boy who entered class on the first day of school with several drawbacks. He had attention deficit hyperactivity disorder (ADHD), was angry with school, had an attitude about learning, and was academically more of a first grader than a second grader. His attitude was "try to teach me if you can." This boy, however, was very mechanically minded; his father was a mechanic, and he was raised around garage operations.

He had been referred to Special Ed. In the early part of the school year, it was decided that due to his behavior, his ADHD and lack of focus, and his academic needs, he would be in Special Ed most of the day. I asked to keep him in my classroom during math, with the stipulation that if he refused to work in class, I could send him back. I knew Johnny really liked being with the other children in the classroom.

At first, Johnny gave me a hard time during math class because he expected to use computers at will and not have to do any of the workbook or worksheet exercises. I established the rules: He needed to complete the workbook, same as the other students; however, I would modify his work on the worksheets. He tried bargaining his way out of his work, but I stood firm. Johnny learned to complete his workbook. Extra help was available to him anytime he needed it. He started completing parts of the worksheets.

I asked for his input when I made special computer-generated worksheets for him and gave him choices on the difficulty of the assignment, how many items to put on a page, and how large a font to use (he liked the largest font). Slowly, Johnny finished his math workbook with less and less complaining, and he completed the computer-generated math worksheets I made just for him.

When his written work was done, he was assigned to a math computer program. His math skills improved by leaps and bounds. After a few months, Johnny could add, subtract, carry (regroup), and borrow. He took a real liking to computers, so I showed him how to do some light computer troubleshooting. He was able to help others with their computer problems. He was the first in class to turn the computers off properly, and he promptly put himself in charge of making sure all students took good care of their stations. Johnny's self-esteem improved tremendously; he got along with his peers and became a much happier child. I credit the use of computers with motivating him and allowing him to specialize in an area that wouldn't have been available to him in a computer-free classroom.

There have been so many benefits to using computers in the classroom. Computers have generated tremendous excitement in my classroom and helped motivate slow-working students. Students master their addition and subtraction facts painlessly, as they do computation facts in larger quantities than they could ever complete on paper.

Perfectionists prefer to make mistakes on a computer, rather than see erasures or checkmarks on their papers. A computer is a safe tool for students who are not risk takers. As a result, it's easy to challenge my second graders to attempt multiplication facts, division, or other third-grade skills. By the end of the school year, most students have mastered their second-grade skills at a much higher level than was possible in the past. It makes the transition to third-grade curriculum easier. Students in my class have the opportunity to learn new math skills and to progress as far as they choose.

How has the computer helped me as a teacher? The first weeks of school are particularly challenging as teacher and students adjust to each other. I have had students arrive in my classroom with poor working habits, students identified as having attention deficit disorder (ADD) or ADHD, or some students with poor academic attitudes. When I assign a simple math worksheet with computation, a number of students can't complete even two lines of simple addition or subtraction computation in a one-hour math period. It is very frustrating to teach when students have such poor work habits.

In my early days of teaching, one would have applied consequences to students for such poor performance. My approach today is quite different from what was used 30 years ago. At the beginning of the year, I often modify their assignments. I ask them to complete only what I think they can reasonably complete in one math period. I feel that students develop poor self-esteem when subjected to consequences on a daily basis for not completing class work. Students need to feel success in order to become workers who are willing to take risks. After assigning students math work, I watch them closely.

When I feel they've worked to capacity, I direct them to continue their work on a specific computer math program. Even if a student has not been a diligent worker, I tend to go easy on them those first few months of school. I use the computer as a reward to be granted after their assigned class work is completed. As the weeks go on, I modify less and less, always keeping the computer as the end-of-period assignment. By November, I modify very little. By this time, students have built good work habits and are finishing their math work on time because they are anxious to work on a computer.

Technology has helped me tremendously as a teacher in eliminating the negative confrontations one occasionally has in the classroom. I seldom keep students in at recess to complete math work or even have to assign it for homework. The problem of unfinished work has fixed itself because of the computer assignments. All students in my class enjoy math because of the user-friendly technology that's available during most math periods.

Throughout the year, I vary the math programs and assignments. Students who need more drilling with specific concepts are assigned those drills on a computer. Students who want to be challenged with multiplication or division have the opportunity to progress as much as they choose. Individualization becomes manageable. Included on the math Web site are "teacher tools," which I sometimes assign. Students can create their own math worksheets and, on occasion, correct their own work. I monitor and keep track of what they do. Students enjoy making choices in their education. When students have a greater say in their learning, they take their education more seriously.

▨ Technology and Discipline

It seems that every year we have more and more students with ADD, ADHD, or even students with serious emotional issues. Left to their own devices, these students can easily take over a classroom with outbursts and disruptions. Computers in the classroom can be a great aid. One year, 50 percent of my students were identified as having ADD or ADHD. Though the first few weeks of school were bumpy—to say the least—by January, the classroom was working very smoothly.

How does one work with disruptive students? One needs to be very patient. Those first months, I teach students tricks for staying on task. I have egg timers available for those who want to time themselves in doing their work, and I place desks in the corners of the classroom where students may choose to go. I lavish praise when they make progress in completing their work. Finally, I always keep the computer as an enticement (for the last class assignment). Distracted students learn to focus so that they can finish their work in a timely manner.

Eventually, all students finish their work on time and earn some math computer time. Midway through the year, my ADD class had calmed down; students were more focused, had developed good work habits, and had learned to finish their assignments on time. Anyone entering my classroom would have had a hard time identifying the ADD students who had been bouncing off the walls and distracting others in August.

Most of all, technology has given everyone in my second-grade class a great love of school. Parents often lament that their child refuses to stay home, even when sick. Having seen the positive effects of technology in the classroom, I could never go back to teaching the old, traditional way. I think that if the computers were not in my classroom, I would look for alternate technology to teach with, such as Math GeoSafari, Electronic *Jeopardy!*, LeapPad, or any of the newer technology games for kids that are available today.

Providing technological math activities as an enticement goes a long way toward motivating students. Best of all, students do their work in a positive atmosphere. Can you think of any other invention that can do so much to motivate, keep students on task, and help you individualize?

Helpful Tips

- Ask for more computers in your classroom. More means you can at least assign a small group of students to work at one time.
- If your school can't afford new computers, send out a note to parents or the community saying you're interested in acquiring old computers to use in your classroom.
- Become computer literate. Take a troubleshooting course so you can handle computer problems or jams in your classroom.
- Apply for grants! Having extra money to spend in your classroom creates excitement for you and the students. It motivates not just the students but also the teacher. You'll be walking with a spring in your step while your peers drag themselves during the school day.

- Be patient with problematic kids. Most have had a hard road to walk in life. Patience and love are free for the giving, and they come back a hundredfold.
- Don't ever be afraid to modify assignments, especially with young students at the beginning of the school year. Modifying builds up their self-confidence and self-esteem. Once they feel better about themselves, they'll take risks and eventually become great students. Remember, modifying is temporary. You should increase the length of the assignments slowly as they improve.
- If your school doesn't have computers, look into different technology. Keep your classes interesting. Ask parents to donate their children's old technology toys. Students love hands-on materials. It breaks up the math routine beautifully.
- If using Internet links in the classroom, don't forget to acquire parents' permission at the beginning of the school year. I explain to parents how we use the computer during a parents' night in the early part of the school year.
- Keep parents abreast of your class curriculum and events by e-mailing them slide shows. Parents always appreciate the extra communication.

CHAPTER 4

Getting Zoned-Out Students to Tune In

Sharon Andrews

Sioux Falls, South Dakota

I t is 8:00 a.m. As I am confronted with a class of 28 fifth graders, most with sleepy eyes and glazed-over looks on their faces, I realize that the task before me—teaching math—is an important one, but it will be challenging under such conditions. How will I connect with the students? How will I be able to engage them in an active learning process? And how will I achieve all of this not only today but for as many days throughout the year as possible when we begin each day with math? This is an intimidating situation for the experienced teacher, not to mention those who may be just getting started.

As if all of this isn't enough, there are other common external factors that often hamper the teacher's ability to energize and connect with the students. In this case, math is the first subject of the day, and I know that some of my students did not get the proper amount of sleep or the proper nutrition before coming to school. Without these basic needs being met, how receptive are the students going to be to my prepared math lesson?

I wonder. I also worry particularly about my fifth-grade girls and their preparation and receptiveness to math for middle school the next year. It is well established that girls tend to lose interest in math as they get older, and as a fifth-grade teacher, I can already begin to see this syndrome affecting my students. In fact, for some of the girls, math is their least favorite subject. Perhaps this contributes to the general impression by some that boys are better in math than girls, but I consider it my mission to do as much as possible to get all my students excited about math. Again, how will I accomplish this in realization of the time of day and the other contributing factors to the students' readiness for learning math?

I have found that the best way to wipe those glazed looks off the children's faces and get them engaged in math is to make the lesson relevant to their own lives. Of course, these are not new words to educators. In fact, many educators have advocated this for years. I concur with the importance of relevance to both the personal and outside worlds, and for math especially, I think relevance is absolutely essential in getting the students mentally engaged and excited.

One manner of relating math to life situations that the students always like to hear is when I share examples from my own personal experiences. In general, children always like to hear about their teacher's personal life, and when I begin to tell such a story, I can immediately see a shift in the entire class from "zoned out" to "tuned in." Further, sharing examples of when I have used math in my own life alleviates the common question, "When are we ever going to use this in our own lives?" I not only illustrate my general use of math in my life, but I always try to share an example that relates specifically to the concept that is being taught. When prompted with my personal accounts, students frequently add their own stories and an invigorating class discussion results that engages all of the students.

For example, recently the math lesson included the objective of finding a percentage of a given number. One activity that almost every child experiences is going out to eat, so I decided to tell a brief story of going to a local restaurant with which the whole class was familiar. I told them the amount of the food bill and how I had to decide how much to tip the waitress, based on the normal 15 percent amount.

An interesting class discussion ensued, and one student volunteered that his family always decided on the amount of the tip based on the quality of the service that his family received. Another child shared with the class that her mother looked at the amount of the tax (6 percent in our state) and then doubled the amount to get close to 15 percent. I then shared that I personally arrive at the amount by taking 10 percent of the bill, which is easy to figure mentally, and then add half of that amount (5 percent) to arrive at 15 percent.

By the time we were finished sharing these stories, the students were interested, awake, and ready to learn. While one might consider this approach as too time-intensive, I consider the time well spent, because the students are more engaged in the learning process and are therefore much more likely to retain the information and feel motivated to incorporate the experiences in their own perception of the concept.

Finally, we must never forget the support of parents at home and in the outside world for adding a further dimension and meaning to the learning process. As a final effort to generalize the use of the concept and encourage students to apply the practice in their own experiences, I challenge parents to become engaged. In my weekly newsletter, I ask parents to let their son or daughter calculate the gratuity the next time they are at a restaurant.

For any math concept in question, there are always opportunities to relate the skill to the teacher's or student's own life, and thus enhance the relevance of math in the outside world. In particular, I consider increasing the relevance to real-life situations to be equally important as other accepted practices, such as using hands-on manipulatives for math instruction. It should be our quest as teachers of math to mount a preemptive and frontal assault on that common question, "When will I ever use this?"

Helpful Tips

- Always show enthusiasm for math. Get very animated. For example, I am the "improper fraction police," and when there is an improper fraction, I blow my whistle. They never forget it.

(Continued)

Helpful Tips (Continued)

- Spend time before the lesson thinking of ways that you can share your own life experiences to make the lesson more relevant. Bring visual aids from home, if appropriate.
- Have students think of ways that the math concept could relate to their own lives. This anticipates and attacks the questions, "Why do we have to learn this?" and "When will I ever use this?"
- Encourage students to think on their own. Refrain from "spoon-feeding." Reassure the students that everyone struggles at one time or another. I believe that students often think that all mathematics should be easy and that they may be the only child in the class who struggles. They should be told that difficulties are a common aspect of life in general. Challenges at school help prepare them for other struggles.
- Have a positive attitude about math. Really get excited when the students have challenging problems to work out. Equate challenging problems to situations like "working a puzzle."
- Talk with parents about displaying positive attitudes about math at home. Share your concerns with them often.

CHAPTER 5

Letting Student Strengths Lead Math Problem Solving

Steven Wyborney

Nyssa, Oregon

Mathematical problem solving can be an area of concern for some teachers. Long-form assessments require students to demonstrate conceptual understanding, well-chosen and accurately executed processes, mathematical communication, and a defense of the given solution. Arming students for these assessments and—far more important— for the mathematical needs of real life can seem like a daunting task to many teachers. However, it does not have to be difficult at all, especially when students are fully involved in the instructional process.

The most important step in guiding student growth is to fully value the creativity, experience, and extraordinary learning potential of each child. Give the students full credit for their astonishing learning capacity, and recognize their potential to impact one another.

In order to launch student input into the problem-solving process, begin with a question. It is important to let the question lead the lesson because it represents both possibility and opportunity while providing the students with freedom to explore. Select a rich question, preferably one that can ignite several paths to a single solution. Then provide each student with a clear overhead transparency and an overhead marker, and allow each of them to dabble with the problem.

Here is a sample problem:

> The power company just put in eight new power poles. However, somebody made a mistake. Instead of setting them in a straight line, they were all set in a circle. The wires are also mixed up. In fact, every pole is connected directly to every other pole with a single wire. How many wires did the power company use?

When the students have had time to generate solutions, begin inviting them one at a time to bring their work up, placing it on the overhead projector for everyone to see. Immediately take on the role of a "captor and clarifier of ideas." Identify strategies that students are using. Praise students for sharing, and value each student's perspective and creativity. You may need to provide correction or clarification throughout the process, but maintain the concept that there may be many paths to a correct answer and that exploration and comparison of a variety of paths are highly valued.

After several students have shared their strategies, immediately present another problem with a similar concept, and allow students to respond using any of the strategies that have been presented. Some students will want to use their original strategy, while others will be attracted to one of the new strategies or styles that they have just encountered. A few may try multiple strategies or again try to invent a new approach. You will be surprised at how quickly students acquire one another's strategies.

At this point in the lesson, you may feel a strong sense of success. You may even feel that the lesson has strongly achieved an initial goal, so that you are ready to take over and steer the refinement of the ideas. Resist this urge. Instead, ask the students to develop and refine their own ideas.

One of the most successful approaches I've taken at this point is to ask the students to develop math television shows that feature multiple solutions to a single problem. Working in small groups that focus on unique problems, students carefully analyze the question, brainstorm solutions, and decide how they will articulate and defend their solutions to an audience. Because television is highly visual, students must find ways to illustrate or animate their answers. The series of steps they follow will be highly similar to the ones that they will face in an assessment and, more important, in a real-life situation.

As students decide how to craft scripts, present the problem, and explain and articulate solutions, I lend support with technical issues that could slow or interfere with their learning. While the process may be organic, the need for refinement, clarity, and conciseness is provided by a time frame, typically no more than five minutes. Using purposeful animation, the students bring their solutions to life, supported by their most articulate mathematical reasoning. Typically, students fully and very impressively connect the prompt to a discovered solution, which they explain and defend.

As you might guess, the crowning moment of the process is when the videos are shown to the whole class. Although much of the greatest value has already been attained, this moment drives the process. In addition, because groups have been working on a variety of types of problems, all students learn from one another's presentations. They often discover distinctions and similarities on their own.

If you repeat the process, you will find that the intensity of your students' focus will turn toward how they can best understand and explain their solutions. They will have moved beyond simply seeking the answer—instead, they will be concerned with the articulation of the mathematics that is driven by the question. That is the goal of the problem-solving design, and that is one of your primary goals as well.

Encourage your students to have fun and to embrace mathematical problem solving with creativity and expression. They will thoroughly enjoy the opportunity and freedom to refine and express mathematical ideas. I am sure they will surprise you with a rich variety of strategies. They are, after all, extraordinary learners.

Helpful Tips

■ Recognize that at the completion of the process, you will have set your class up for one of the simplest and most powerful reviews of problem-solving strategies possible. When you show the tapes to the students in the future, and they experience the sensation of teaching themselves, the full value of the experience will return to them.

■ To heighten the interest of the projects, I like to announce to the entire school a time when the videos will be shown over our schoolwide network. One day before the videos are aired, I e-mail the problem to every teacher in the school so that, if they wish, they can present it to their students before viewing the videos.

■ In some circumstances, you may find value in providing the students with the answer to the problem before they begin. This will immediately shift the focus of the task from finding the answer to discovering and analyzing useful strategies.

CHAPTER 6

Using Animated Learning Icons to Capture and Enhance Instruction

Steven Wyborney

Nyssa, Oregon

O ne of my favorite strategies in teaching mathematics is to develop a learning icon that accompanies each and every lesson. A learning icon is an animated representation of the entirety of the task analysis of the lesson.

Simply put, whenever I teach a new lesson, I create an animated illustration of the lesson. That illustration, which I simply call a learning icon, serves to represent the experience of learning from that lesson. The result is that when I present the learning icon to the students during any of the days following the lesson, they are able to vividly recall and interact with a specific instance of prior learning. Instead of tying into prior lessons with phrases such as "Remember when we learned how to add decimals yesterday?" I show a succinct animation that clearly illustrates the entire motion of aligning decimals and completing operations.

Much as one family member might say to another, "Remember our trip to Yellowstone?"—a question sure to evoke memories and to spark conversation based on shared experience—a learning icon evokes a group learning experience. However, it is more effective than a simple phrase. Imagine how much more effective a photograph of the Yellowstone trip might be at capturing an experience and evoking precise memories.

The clear details, the specific example, and the moment caught in that photograph represent a specific memory and launch many other attached memories. Now consider how much more effective a precisely focused video clip, in combination with a well-chosen photograph, would be compared to the very broad phrase, "Remember our trip to Yellowstone?"

Learning icons are precise captures of learning experiences that can be reviewed, modified, adapted, and extended. While I normally retain the original format of the icon, which is based on a shared learning experience, I find that it is necessary to change the content within the icon. The animated learning icons then become powerful questioning tools specifically tailored so that students can immediately interact with content from prior learning experiences in order to seek and synthesize new connections.

As a fourth- to fifth-grade looping teacher, I have developed learning icons for virtually every concept that is covered in the state and national standards for these grades. One of the most fascinating benefits of using learning icons is that their ready access allows me to compare concepts when I normally would not have time or opportunity to do so. For example, in the fourth grade, you might not normally have the opportunity to compare the area of a parallelogram to the specific measures of its interior angles. However, using learning icons, it is very easy to display these two distinct concepts simultaneously and to allow students to explore the issue.

The wealth of opportunities for exploring mathematical concepts and for students to synthesize abounds when I use learning icons. Many of my math concept lessons focus on as many as 40 distinct concepts and the relationships among those concepts.

Clearly, the value of learning icons depends on the teacher's ability to identify the heart of the lesson and then to be able to illustrate it with precise animation. This is not an easy thing to do, and it does take practice. However, the eventual benefits in terms of time and student learning are well worth it.

Another surprising benefit of developing animated learning icons, which represent the task analysis of a captured learning experience, is that they provide a clear means for discussing instructional strategies with other educators. In addition, because the learning icons are normally very "light" in terms of computer memory, it is quite simple to e-mail them to other classrooms throughout the nation, or beyond. It is heartening to know that an effective instructional development in Oregon can very easily, and quite rapidly, be provided to teachers and their students throughout the nation and could serve to support their education as well.

Currently I have developed well over 2,000 high-quality, refined learning icons. I am rapidly discovering that these icons are highly useful in other classrooms throughout the nation. This realization has led me to think in much broader terms as a teacher, and I believe that it has improved my instruction.

I would encourage educators with an interest in animation to try developing an effective learning icon that captures a learning experience. You will have a good sense that you have been successful if your icon evokes the prior learning experience and simultaneously opens new possibilities.

Helpful Tips

- If a student ever follows a lesson with the phrase "I don't get it," pay careful attention to your response. Your tendency may be to seek out the misunderstanding and succinctly sum up the heart of the lesson. In doing so, you may be providing the background narrative or a learning icon. Build from opportunities such as these, turning them into rich moments of understanding. Then capture those moments of clarification.

(Continued)

Helpful Tips (Continued)

- Concentrate the development of your icon on the understanding of the concept rather than the appearance of the icon.
- Use only purposeful animation. There are many animations available designed to enhance presentations, but their effect is nearly always distraction. Some animations serve the concept with precise purpose. Identify and use those icons.

CHAPTER 7

Honoring the Middle School Student

Heather Sullivan

Albuquerque, New Mexico

In casual conversation, when I share that I am a middle school mathematics teacher, I often receive responses like, "I could never do that. God bless you." Sometimes the person makes a face as though a very pungent and surprising aroma just swept through the room. "That must be tough. Middle schoolers can be very difficult." I usually agree that my job is challenging, but then I make the point that being in middle school is what is really difficult.

Perhaps it is more understandable to most people why a teacher would have an affinity for the lower grades or the upper grades. Very young students are indisputably cute and tend to adore their teachers. Helping young children to discover the world of reading, for example, has an almost visceral appeal for many people. I certainly do not mean to imply that the elementary school teacher's job is easier, just that it seems to have a more universal pull.

Drawing in other teachers, high school students reach a level of intellectual, social, and emotional maturity that allows for very impressive work. They accomplish things athletically, artistically, and academically that are rightly considered adult achievements. Yet some teachers do love and indeed prefer teaching somewhere in between. Why would that be? I hope to share my answer to that question, as middle school students have captured my heart.

Consider the possibility that middle school students are too often characterized by what they cannot do instead of what they can, by what they are not instead of what they are. It is true that these young people are not a lot of things. They are not children. They are not adults. What they are, though, is quite amazing; and they are best appreciated and understood when we teach and relate to them based on what they are instead of what they are not.

Middle school students often have surprisingly strong abilities, and they often have equally strong needs. First and foremost, the unique and capable students who occupy our middle schools desperately need us to understand that they are not simply overgrown, rebellious versions of elementary school students, nor are they smallish, awkward versions of high school students.

They have much to offer if we take the time and care to reach them at their level, rather than looking down at them or asking them to meet us at our level. Middle school students are very sensitive to condescension, and they do not tend to give their best when treated like young children. On the other hand, they are not adults and are likely to disappoint teachers who expect consistently mature behavior.

Middle school students also tend to be highly emotional, even if they spend a lot of energy hiding or disguising their emotions. These young people are undergoing major physical changes, including dramatic neurological changes, and emotions can go along for the ride. Is it any wonder that these students seem inconsistent from our adult perspective?

Middle school teachers who attempt to hold students' emotions at bay, who discourage any social interaction in the classroom, are fighting an uphill battle. I believe we should acknowledge and respect the overwhelming importance of social interactions in the lives of these students, though this does not mean students' emotions and social nature should have the upper hand.

Classroom management is essential, and a socially healthy atmosphere is manageable. In my experience, middle school teachers who invest time and energy in establishing a classroom culture of respect and safety, in which emotions and social interactions are acknowledged and guided, tend to be very happy with the return on their investment.

Brain-based research tells us that helping students develop emotional connections to the concepts they encounter in school will aid in retention. Cooperative activity and play are two ways to acknowledge and tap into student emotions in the math classroom. Your typical middle school students have not forgotten the importance of play, and arm-twisting is rarely necessary.

Teachers looking for students who are eager to participate—and who are also ready to begin incorporating more sophisticated rules and strategies into their play—will not be disappointed in the middle school classroom. Mathematics is a subject well suited for play, despite the traditional approach toward teaching it. Teachers who actively connect the inherent playfulness of mathematics and of middle school students are likely to meet success.

The mind of a middle school student is fascinating, in part because it is in the process of learning to juggle the concrete with the abstract. From sarcasm to symbolism, the world opens up to new and exciting possibilities. Compound that shifting reality by introducing middle school students to algebra, the realm in which mathematics itself becomes abstract, and you are in for some excitement. I love introducing my seventh graders to the world of variables and equations.

I love helping them develop greater mathematical confidence, even as the material grows more difficult. These students are at the crux of developing their identities, forming their mathematical self-concepts, and deciding what they like and what they believe. I am currently hooked on teaching in middle school because I believe it is a venue through which I can make positive and lasting impacts on how people perceive and respect themselves, their capabilities, and their world.

In a sense, I believe this comes down to honoring middle school students. They deserve our respect. They get up each day to courageously face the reality of their changing minds, changing bodies, and changing identities. While many adults are glad to have forgotten what that adolescent reality felt like, some of us still feel very connected to it. I am certain that the struggles feel as real as ever to today's middle school students.

I try to validate my students' feelings and to support them in dealing with their changing realities. Simultaneously, I set high standards for my students, and I expect a great deal from them as their math teacher. I try to find a certain balance, challenging myself to be both empathetic and demanding. When I hit that balance, I know in my heart why I am working with middle school students.

Helpful Tips

- Attend school plays and sports events to support your students' interests outside of the classroom.
- Start the year by asking students to brainstorm topics that might connect their interests to mathematics (for example, music, car mechanics, or origami). Then, challenge yourself to incorporate some of those topics into the year.
- Assign individual, creative projects (for example, posters, presentations, or models) that allow students to explore topics that you will not have time to incorporate into your formal curriculum. These can be done mostly outside of class if you provide a longer time period.
- Assign optional challenge work for students who excel.
- Use informal, anonymous surveys to learn how students feel about certain lessons and activities. Incorporate their feedback into your planning.
- Remember that you are more than a mathematics teacher and that they are more than mathematics students.

CHAPTER 8

Sweet Solutions in Math Make a Difference in the World

Pam Roller

Galveston, Indiana

M y second-grade class has run a business called Chocolate Lollipops, Inc., since 1999. The students became young entrepreneurs, and they were able to apply their basic math skills to a real-life situation. Once a month, chocolate lollipops were made into seasonal or holiday shapes and sold for 50 cents each. The money earned was given to a charitable cause or to someone less fortunate.

The students had various jobs to teach them about responsibility, teamwork, and how to get along in a real-world job situation. The students delivered order forms to each classroom in our school so we would know how much chocolate and how many sticks and bags were needed to make the lollipops. The students would have to tally the results. They had to be able to read the information off the order forms in order to be able to tally.

They witnessed the process of solids being made into liquids as the chocolate was melted and poured into the plastic candy molds. Then they watched liquids become solids again when the molds were put in the freezer to harden the chocolate into the holiday or seasonal shapes. The molds had cavities in various shapes to hold the chocolate. Some molds had six cavities, and we had four of these molds.

It was a neat way to teach multiplication. My students quickly learned that 4 times 6 was 24, and that it was much faster to use four molds than to use only one mold four different times. My students learned many of their multiplication tables by making lollipops. We had a mold that had only three race car cavities and we had six of these molds, which made 18 race cars at a time.

Being from Indiana, home of the Indianapolis 500, it was cool to end the year with an order for race cars. One year we received a huge order from ITT Corporation in Indianapolis for a thousand race cars. Needless to say, it took parental involvement to carry out this order. My class was called SMILES, INC., and we gave the $500 earned to Operation Smile so that a disfigured child would have the opportunity to have a real smile in life.

Some months we would offer two or three different kinds of lollipops so our customers would have a choice. This was great because it gave us an opportunity to graph the results, make comparisons, and practice figuring out which kind sold the most or the least. My students learned firsthand about money by collecting, sorting, counting, and making change. They had opportunities to work two- and three-digit problems in addition and subtraction through our lollipop business.

My class learned how to partner in the world as well. One month we earned only $75. That didn't seem like much, but when we decided to give it to the Wheelchair Foundation, they matched our $75 so that a little girl in San Salvador could have a wheelchair. My students received a certificate and a photo of the little girl we helped to get a wheelchair. She even had a smile on her face!

In May of 2004, my second graders sold chocolate race car lollipops during their lunchtime to everyone in our school. They earned $100, and it was given as a scholarship to a graduating high school senior in our school district. Over the years, my students have given their chocolate lollipop earnings to many charitable causes, including The Ronald McDonald House, Make-a-Wish Foundation, St. Jude Children's Research Hospital, The March of Dimes, and more.

Once a young, 24-year-old farmer lost his arm in a farming accident. We sold 600 lollipops so we could give him $300. That was a defining moment for my students. It was a lesson you could never get from a textbook. The young farmer came to my class and told how he lost his arm. He also told my students that it would not stop him from doing what he wanted to do in life. He would just have to learn to do things in a new way! We will never forget that experience.

In 2003, my second graders made lollipops and sent them as a random act of kindness to someone on every continent around the world. A missionary in Cali, Colombia, to whom we had sent lollipops was coming to Indiana to renew her status as a missionary and contacted us to see if she could visit our class. Arrangements were made, and my students were treated to the unforgettable experience of a lifetime.

The missionary brought memorabilia, souvenirs, photographs, and more, and even brought special foods for my students to try. She brought my students miniature magnetic handmade baskets of vegetables from her country. She gave my class several handmade wooden string toys and games that children play in Cali, including yo-yos, assorted spinning tops, and a gyroscope. My students were also given beautiful handmade bracelets. The missionary brought a can of candy for the children to try. It looked like a topping we would put on ice cream, but in Cali, people eat it with a tiny little tasting stick similar to the wooden ice-cream sticks we have in the United States. The missionary shared a nice scrapbook of her schoolchildren in Grades K through 5 doing many activities so my students could see what schoolchildren do in Colombia. My students were fascinated with her visit. The adventure continued because the missionary and I had our students write to each other the following school year.

We didn't make any money that time, but in any business, it pays to be kind and generous. We had no idea that a simple act of kindness could lead to such an extraordinary experience.

During the 2004–2005 school year, my students decided to use the lollipop earnings for the whole year to establish a memorial scholarship fund for two boys from our school district who lost their lives in 2004 battling cystic fibrosis. The teenage boys were brothers a year apart in age. In May of 2005, the father of the boys and the recipient of the scholarship came to visit my second-grade class. The girl selected for the scholarship had overcome many obstacles in her life.

She had gone through numerous surgeries. She had to cope with a full-body cast more than once during her school-age years. School was difficult for her, and it was a challenge to deal with everything physically, mentally, emotionally, and socially. The girl struggled to the point that she was not sure if she should even consider going to college.

Needless to say, she was moved to tears when my second graders presented her with a $600 scholarship. It was a wonderful way to honor the memory of two special young boys and give someone an opportunity to further her education. The girl attended college the fall semester, has been doing great, and is loving it!

Helpful Tip

■ I have found that while I'm teaching the basics in math, students learn the most when the teacher chooses to integrate the curriculum. Students remember more and understand better when they are personally involved, included, and engaged in the learning process. Ultimately, students need to apply what they have learned to a real-life situation. They should also learn the importance of trying to make a little difference in the world, too.

CHAPTER 9

But . . . Does It Make Sense?

Patricia F. Clark

Elmont, New York

When I graduated from elementary school, I received the award for mathematics. I had achieved something no other graduate that year had . . . 100 percent in every quarterfinal math test. But what did I really know?

I really knew how to compute quickly and accurately. I really knew long division, percentages, and fractions—but beyond that, I knew I was on shaky ground. I had difficulty spotting extraneous information in word problems. I was often confused about the number and order of steps to take in problems that I knew had to be multistep. I questioned myself about which step ultimately yielded the answer. I never asked myself, "Does this make sense?" because the frightening answer was, "No."

In high school, I didn't fare much better. I remember feelings of anxiety that I would be called upon and would feel foolish if I didn't have the answer, or if I did have it, could I explain how I had gotten it?

I remember tears and tutors. Luckily, in college I had no required math courses. The closest I got to it there was my roommate, who was a math major!

When I decided to become an elementary teacher, one of my first methods courses was . . . math. Here it was my pleasure to meet one of the finest teachers I had ever had. He broke math down into reasonable chunks, he made it fathomable, he offered strategies for finding solutions, and, most important, he gave positive feedback. I finally became less anxious, and when my head cleared, I found that I was not afraid to make mistakes and I was actually able to solve many problems on my own.

There were times in the class when the teacher purposely frustrated us so that we would understand how children who don't understand math feel. That was an all too familiar feeling for me. I vowed then that I would be the best, most understanding math teacher I could be so that children in my class would never feel as I had. I have worked doubly hard to understand where children's thought processes are breaking down. These are some steps I have taken to assure solid learning and understanding.

A planned, sequential, and cumulative review is essential. In this type of spiral, children will continually see and practice all phases of math until they are mastered. Nothing is ever left to chance, nothing is ever truly gone . . . it recycles! Those who struggle will always have a chance to learn what they may have missed.

It also allows a student who has mastered a skill to move on to the next level of that skill in isolation or as it is used in conjunction with other skills. Finally, a cumulative review is a window into children's thinking and serves as an informal assessment. It plays a role in identifying skills that need to be revisited, thus allowing us to form smaller homogeneous or cooperative groups for that purpose. As children see skills again, they are more likely to internalize them so that they can be used as the foundation for higher-order skills. I must stress again that this type of review must be well planned and flexible.

Math journal writing is a necessary component for any well-rounded mathematician. This is a process that evolves. In the youngest grades, children draw and give verbal explanations. As they acquire more writing skills, they should still verbalize thoughts, which can then be converted into simple written statements.

This is an ongoing process that requires thoughtful modeling. In the beginning, the verbalizations and writing can be done together to provide a sample that children can use in the subsequent writings they will do on their own. Here again, journal writing is a window into children's thinking. This metacognitive aspect is crucial for children of any age. The earlier children learn to think about their own thinking, the better!

Another activity that excites children and motivates them is a daily problem. Many textbook publishers use this component in their series. If not, teachers can create these problems on their own. Children can use a part of each day to solve the problem alone or with partners. Problems can center on any of the concepts that have been taught or can challenge children to think about and develop hypotheses before they are introduced. An outgrowth of this activity has also been that the children want to create problems of their own to challenge each other. They also plan and write math mini-books, which we keep in a book basket. I have found that these child-created books are very popular. The children love to borrow and read each other's books.

Manipulatives are a key element in every math class. These allow children to bring the abstract to a more concrete level. They also encourage students to solve problems in less conventional, more constructivist ways. I find that allowing children to use these materials in "free time" helps create a comfort level with them prior to using them in purely instructional scenarios.

A final key ingredient in successful math teaching, I think, is helping children to know when something does not make sense. We always do this when we teach children to read. It is a form of self-monitoring behavior that separates strong readers from weaker ones. The question "Does this make sense?" allows children to stop, reflect, and reevaluate their own progress and try to deduce where their comprehension of the problem is breaking down. Once again, this is an evolving process. First, children must know what they know or don't know, and then they must have strategies to fix it. These must be carefully taught and modeled.

Math is serious business, a tool for a lifetime. It can and should be taught in an atmosphere that is conducive to exploration, one free from as much stress as possible. It should be fun, a subject in which children can enjoy the use of different methods to solve the same problem, a subject where teachers encourage creativity and self-expression. When math spills into all areas of classroom life, not just math time, children begin to understand how useful and widespread it is in their young lives. An even bigger bonus would be cooperative planning among the art, gym, and music teachers. This would make math come alive!

Helpful Tips

- Use a well-planned, sequential, and cumulative review.
- Teach and encourage journal writing in math.
- Plan some type of daily problem that challenges the mind and encourages the development of alternate strategies for an ultimate solution.
- Develop a comfort level with manipulatives early on in the process.
- Encourage children to be metacognitive and to ask the question "Does it make sense?" with strategies to use if it does not.
- Use opportunities throughout the school day to reinforce concepts previously taught.

CHAPTER 10

Keeping Math Alive After State Testing

Dianne M. Peterson

Satellite Beach, Florida

O ur state testing, the Florida Comprehensive Assessment Test (FCAT), takes place in late February and early March. From August to the day testing begins, we are literally filling our students' heads with test strategies, which are taught through our Sunshine State Standards.

The push to teach the key content in our curriculum prior to the test always leaves parents and students thinking that after testing the school year is complete. My job as the math teacher for all the fifth graders at our school is to continue to engage the students in content that will provide a deeper understanding of the fifth-grade mathematical concepts and ensure mastery of the Sunshine State Standards. This is not easy, as spring fever and the "I am almost a sixth grader syndrome" also strike.

A way to keep them motivated and to continue to make math fun is by celebrating Pi Day (March 14). A note is sent home to parents a week prior to Pi Day, enlisting their help in providing snacks that are circular in shape. These snacks are the materials we use to explore circumference and discover the value of pi. Of course, after using the food items as our units of measurement, the best part is being able to eat your "math tools." We make a human circle composed of the entire fifth grade and use a rope to simulate the diameter of the circle. The book *Sir Cumference and the Dragon of Pi* is read to the students.

I wear a "pi-rate" T-shirt, and one of the students' challenges is to create a pi picture. These are completed prior to Pi Day and decorate the hallway. This activity engages students of all abilities in a meaningful and delicious celebration of pi. *Food* and *fun* make for a great math event!

Helpful Tip

- I continually assess the students' mastery of a concept with four-problem mini-quizzes. After scoring them, I can quickly identify who has mastered the concept. These students become the trainers and meet with the students who are the "trainees," those needing more practice. Everyone strives to be a trainer.

CHAPTER 11

Teaching and Learning Math Vocabulary With Meaning

Debbie Gordon

Phoenix, Arizona

My dilemma was how to teach my third graders math vocabulary words that would be meaningful and useful for them to know. The national and state math standards require students to "Use grade-level appropriate mathematical terminology." In the past, I had students use their math journals to write down the name of each term, the definition, and then give an example for each term. I found this to be not very effective, useful, or meaningful for my students, especially when it came to standardized test time.

I started the following year by changing how I talked to my students about mathematics. When I wanted them to remember a new vocabulary word, I would ask them to explain its meaning to me using their own natural language and then have a student (instead of me) demonstrate the term by showing an example to the rest of the class.

This was better already, as the teaching and learning shifted from me doing the talking to the students sharing what they had learned. I then added three little words that seemed to connect the meaning of each word with the importance of learning it. I would say, "Mathematicians call this . . ." My students loved hearing the word "mathematician," and whenever I used it, they knew it meant something very important for them to know.

We started off the year reviewing adding two-digit numbers together. I told my boys and girls that "mathematicians call the answer to adding numbers together the sum," and they made a collective "Ooooh." No one had ever talked to them about mathematicians before, and it made them all feel very important to know the language that "real" mathematicians used. They never forgot the meaning of the word "sum" that year. It had worked!

Throughout the rest of that year, we learned the meaning of difference, quotient, divisor, product, numerator, denominator, and more through the words of mathematicians. The students learned the required vocabulary of third-grade mathematics with interest, ease, and meaning. They were able to use them accurately and confidently throughout the year as well as on the required standardized tests. I have continued to use this "teaching tip" for many years with students from first grade through sixth grade, and they all continue to be amazed and interested in what "real" mathematicians do and say.

same idea is useful when simplifying fractions, since that process is really factoring out the same factor from both the numerator and the denominator.

Students will notice those fractions whose numerator is larger than the denominator. One such example would be a birthday of November 8, $\frac{11}{8}$. I find that students often can tell me that this is an improper fraction but have not attached meaning to that vocabulary term. Through discussion and illustration, I want the students to recognize that this type of fraction represents more than one whole. Many students will also provide the definition of a mixed number at this point by offering that $\frac{11}{8}$ equals $1\frac{3}{8}$.

The next part of the discussion with the class will focus on the strategies the students used to line themselves up. Usually at this point, students will say that they decided whether their fraction was more or less than $\frac{1}{2}$. This reflects students who are using the relationship that exists between the numerator and the denominator. Some groups used cross products to check individual pairs of fractions. Students also drew pictures to determine the size of their fraction compared with another fraction.

1. Name any fractions that need to be simplified.

2. Name any fractions whose value is greater than one.

3. Make a model comparing any two of these fractions.

4. Write a number line using these fractions in order from least to greatest.

CHAPTER 14

A Systematic Approach to Factoring Trinomials

Jim Miller

Cle Elum, Washington

Suggested experiments to collect data:

Diameter, Circumference

- Measure and record the diameter and the circumference of eight different-size circular objects. (Linear and the slope should be 3.14.)

Diameter, Volume

- Measure and record the diameter and volume of different-size spheres (balls). Measure the volume by noting the displacement of water in a beaker or graduated cylinder of water caused by immersing the ball (waffle balls won't work). (Cubic and constant is pi/6.)

▧ Table Roll—Measure Time, Distance, Galileo

- Measure and record the time and distance a marble (or some other round object that will roll straight) rolls down a slightly inclined table. Galileo did this and conjectured that the steeper the incline, the more the object would roll in the pattern of a falling object, and from that was able to model falling objects. (Constant will vary with the slope of the table and the object being rolled, but the model will be quadratic.)

▧ Divided Cords in a Sphere

- Using The Geometer's Sketchpad or drawing a circle, locate an arbitrary point, draw several cords (on The Geometer's Sketchpad, just move one), and measure each section of the cord from the point to the circle. (Model will be an inverse variation.)

▧ Grocery Ads

- Ads for hamburger give cost per pound. Enter the cost for several different amounts. Discuss the nature of the domain-continuous and -positive.
- Ads for soft drinks are per six-pack, for example. Enter the cost for several different amounts. Discuss the nature of the domain-discrete.

▧ Ball Bounce

- Drop a ball from different heights and measure and record the drop height and the corresponding bounce.

▧ Squares in a Rectangle

- Record the different length and width dimensions of rectangles that have an area of 48 square units.

▧ Pendulum

- Record the period for different lengths of a pendulum arm. Be sure to gather data for very short lengths.

Balloon Sled

- Record the balloon diameter and the distance a balloon sled travels. Use straws for a nozzle, a 3 × 5 card, and a straw on the fishing line.

Pennies on a Meter Stick

- Place a meter stick with the 18-inch mark at the edge of the table. Stack pennies on the ruler 2 inches from the edge of the desk until it falls. Record 2 inches and the number of pennies. Repeat for several increments of 2 inches from the desk edge.

Rubber Band Scale

- Hang weights on the end of a rubber band and record how much increase in length is produced for various weights (Hooke's Law).

Card Lab One

- Hold a card at arm's length, one arm's length from a wall. With one eye closed, note the width of the spot on the wall that is blocked from view. Move the card to two, three, four, and so on arm's lengths from the wall and record the widths hidden and the corresponding arm's lengths the card is from the wall.

Card Lab Two

- A card is held at one arm's length from the wall and kept there. As in Card Lab One, note the width covered on the wall with the eye at various arm's lengths from the card. Suggested arm's lengths between the eye and the card are one, two, three, four, one half, and one quarter.

Sign Bracket

- Tape two meter sticks together a half inch from the ends. Wrap a string around one of the exposed half-inch ends of the meter stick. Tie a small weight to one end of the string. Tie a loop on the other end about one foot up. Using a spring scale, measure the force required to hold the meter sticks up when the string is straight up, 10 degrees from straight up, and 20, 30, 40, 50, 60, 70, 80, 85, and 87 degrees from straight up.

▨ Balloon Hemisphere Surface Area

- Find a balloon that when it's inflated with various amounts of air, the end appears to be a hemisphere. When it is relatively small, use a ballpoint pen to draw approximations of square centimeters on the hemisphere portion to estimate the surface area. Record the radius and the surface area. Increase the radius, measure it, and find the average area of one square and estimate the surface area. Repeat for other radii.

▨ Weight of Similar Shapes

- Find several similar shapes, such as pieces of wood doweling whose length is equal to its diameter. Measure and record the diameters of the dowels to the nearest millimeter, and record their weights to the nearest tenth of a gram.

▨ Friction

- Make a loop of string. Slip it between the middle pages of a textbook so that a spring scale can be hooked in the loop. Drag the book across the desktop at a constant rate. Record the force required to drag the book. Stack an identical book on the first and record the force required to drag the two. Drag three, four, and five books and record the force required.

▨ Standing Waves in a Long Spring

- Create a fundamental wave on a long spring. Record the frequency and the wavelength. Keeping the same distance apart, create the first harmonic (one node), and record the wavelength and frequency. Continue with three nodes, four, five, and so on.

Constant Perimeter on a Rectangle

- Tie a piece of string about 2 feet in length into a loop. Placing it on graph paper, create various rectangles. Record the widths and the areas.

Dice Roll

- Pick a number (or two). Roll the dice 10 times and record how many times the chosen number(s) showed. Record for 20, 30, 40, 50 rolls, and so on.

Circle Area

- Draw circles of various radii on graph paper. Use the squares on the graph paper to estimate the areas of the circles. Record the radii and areas.

Balloon Volume

- Add one breath to a balloon. Measure the diameter. Add another approximately equal breath. Measure the diameter again, and so on. Record the number of breaths and the diameters.

In every experiment, it is important to remove horizontal translations of data by making sure that the data has a "good zero." For example, in the balloon volume experiment, remove the unpressurized balloon's diameter. For the table roll, start timing when the ball starts to roll, and roll the ball from a zero.

CHAPTER 15

Engaged Students Love Math

Donna H. Henry

Chandler, Arizona

My goal each year is that my students will love to study mathematics as much as I love to teach it. I take that responsibility very seriously and work hard each year to find new and innovative ideas to bring to each concept. One of the most engaging units I teach is the area and perimeter concepts of our measurement unit. Measurement is an important math topic, because the processes learned help students master other concepts such as geometry, number sense and fractions, patterns, and data analysis.

By the fourth grade, students are ready to broaden their understanding and use of measurement to other attributes, such as the area and perimeter of shapes, rather than just measuring the lengths of objects. They are also ready to begin to develop and use formulas to measure those attributes. I have compiled and/or created several activities and projects over the past few years that have been successful in helping my students meet the national standards for measurement, geometry, algebra, problem solving, and communication.

The area and perimeter unit that I have developed by reading articles, participating in workshops, and just by letting the creative juices flow involves the students in several hands-on activities and two major projects. The manipulative activities, both in the classroom and on Web sites, have the students creating and exploring units of measure and discovering the attributes of shapes, as well as measuring. Both of the major projects involve the students in real-life problem-solving applications of the concepts learned.

One goal for this unit is that my students will create their own math knowledge through activities that involve them in explorations and inquiry. It is also my intent that the knowledge gained through the manipulative activities can be applied in solving problems. Math that arises from real-life situations is more relevant to the students' lives. I believe that a concept should grow out of a student's need to know, not just because it is the next chapter in the book.

The National Standard for Problem Solving states that students will ". . . build new mathematical knowledge through problem solving; apply and adapt a variety of appropriate strategies to solve problems; and monitor and reflect on the process of mathematical problem solving . . ." One of my greatest expectations for the outcome of this unit is that the students will see the real-life applications of the concepts learned and will be able to transfer that knowledge to actual problem-solving situations, as well as have fun doing it!

When I begin any unit of study, I do have high expectations for the learning that will take place. Another of my expectations for this area and perimeter component of our measurement unit is that at the end, the students will know the difference between area and perimeter, will know that a defined area can be reconfigured and therefore may have several different perimeters, and will know that measures of perimeters can be depicted as areas other than the original.

I also expect them to discover patterns in areas and perimeters as dimensions of rectangles are doubled, tripled, or even halved. The national standards state that in measurement, the students will ". . . explore what happens to measurements of a two-dimensional shape such as its perimeter and area when the shape is changed in some way; develop strategies for estimating the perimeters (and) areas . . . of irregular shapes; develop, understand, and use formulas to find the area of rectangles."

After a formative assessment, I begin this unit by reviewing the rectangular arrays students created during our multiplication and division unit. We now relate the columns and rows of those arrays to the length and width dimensions of rectangles. The National Standard for Geometry for Grades 3 through 5 states that students will ". . . identify, compare, and analyze attributes of two- and three-dimensional shapes and develop vocabulary to describe those attributes."

As we explore the concept of area, the students make the connection between x times y, which is a product (multiplication fact) and length times width, the result of which is the area of that rectangle. Students are very drawn to technology. Therefore, I use it in many forms in my teaching: PowerPoint presentations, SMART Board activities, Excel spreadsheet applications, and especially, virtual manipulatives. This unit is introduced through a teacher-created PowerPoint presentation, in which the students watch square units combine, rotate, flip, and move to form different configurations and areas.

Using 1-inch color tiles, the students explore various rectangular arrays. We discuss the dimensions of each and the resulting areas to be sure that they understand the relationships. It is important that the students correlate the dimensions to the area and comprehend that area is the total space occupied by the tiles within the dimensions of the rectangle. To grasp the meaning of measurements such as square feet and square yards, the students create a square foot with their color tiles and record the area on a piece of construction paper and cut out the resulting $12'' \times 12''$ squares.

The class is then divided into groups of eight to ten students to create and explore the attributes of a square yard. I give no other formal instructions, because it is exciting to watch as the "lights come on" and students realize one by one that they may not need all the square feet they have or that, in some cases, they may need to "recruit" a square foot from another group. We then record the resulting square yards on large sheets of butcher paper. We then use these tools (the square feet and the square yards) to measure several large areas of our campus. Working in these cooperative groups motivates the students to bounce ideas off one another and learn from each other's mistakes and successes.

Picture books motivate and engage even fourth graders. I often integrate literature selections into my units of study. As a fun extension of the concept of area, I read *One Hundred Hungry Ants* by Elinor J. Pinczes. The students manipulate plastic ants on grid paper to show each of the arrays the ants employ to line up in an orderly fashion. This activity reinforces the concept that rows times columns equals the total square units—in this case, ants—occupying a space.

After checking to be sure that the students understand that area is indeed the total space occupied, we begin to explore and develop the concept of perimeter using a lesson called "Big Gardens, Small Fences" that I read several years ago in the National Council of Teachers of Mathematics (NCTM) publication *Teaching Children Mathematics*. I have numerous children construct on the chalkboard all the rectangular "gardens" for an area of 24 square units using magnetic flowers I made.

They then use magnetic fence sections to surround their gardens and discover that most require a different number of fence pieces. We give the number of fence pieces the measurement name "perimeter." Other students then record on large paper the areas and perimeters and discuss the configuration they believe would make the best garden layout. Not all agree! I allow and encourage my students to develop different strategies for solving problems. These include using manipulative activities, a trial-and-error method, looking for a pattern, or even drawing the problem.

Today's students are growing up in a technology-rich environment and learn in different ways than students did years ago. To be innovative and inventive, I integrate technology into my curriculum in many ways. In addition to introducing new units with teacher-created PowerPoint presentations to stimulate the students' interest and pique their curiosity, I have the students use several Web sites that afford them the opportunities to explore area and perimeter concepts using virtual manipulative activities.

The NCTM Web site (www.nctm.org) is an excellent resource and offers numerous virtual activities. Part of the site lets the students manipulate pattern blocks as I pose situations such as, "If the green triangle has an area of 3 square units, create a design that would have an area of 24 square units, or 52 square units." This activity is great, in that those who find a solution quickly can be asked if they can find another design as well, while I help those who need more guidance.

Students are asked to find the areas and perimeters of irregular shapes at www.shodor.org/interactivate/activities/perimeter/index.html. They count, type in their solutions, and get immediate feedback. Even better, all students can participate in this activity, because the students themselves configure the sizes of the shapes to be calculated, from 2 square units all the way to 100 or more.

In the Reasoning and Proof Standard for Grades 3 through 5, the NCTM expects students in Grades 3 through 5 to "move toward reasoning that depends on relationships and properties," as well as to continually develop, question, and apply conjectures about those mathematical relationships. An innovative teaching tool I employ is a "Growing Shapes" table I created in an Excel spreadsheet program. The students can type in the dimensions of rectangles and see resulting areas and perimeters. This activity helps them see patterns as they double the length and/or width and see the resultant areas and perimeters.

Discovering patterns in this way helps students make connections and gives them a foundation for more abstract concepts later. As the students have more opportunities to look for patterns, and begin to understand that they do not have to count all the squares in an area, but can multiply length times width to get the area of a rectangle and add two lengths and two widths to find the perimeter, I extend this activity to having them create formulas in Excel that will calculate areas and perimeters. It amazes me sometimes that even fourth graders can do that!

The Algebra National Standard for Grades 3 through 5 states that students will "describe, extend, and make generalizations about geometric and numeric patterns; represent and analyze patterns and functions . . . ; investigate how a change in one variable relates to a change in a second variable; model problems with objects and use representations . . ." An activity I implement to accomplish this goal is called "hexominoes," found in the Super Source Color Tiles Kit from the Cuisenaire Company of America (www.etacuisenaire.com/). The students manipulate six color tiles to find all the possible arrangements (hexominoes).

This activity affords my students the opportunity to create irregular shapes and see that the area always remains six square units, and to slide, flip, and turn their shapes to check for congruence. When joined along adjacent sides, the polygon made is also six square units, but the perimeter varies from one polygon to another. This activity helps students learn to organize their findings so that they can keep track of the solutions. Because there are 35 different polygons that can be made, the students sort their resulting polygons and record the perimeters on an Excel spreadsheet. This information is later used to create bar or pie graphs.

Projects connect classroom learning to real-life experiences. The first major project in this unit is one in which the students formulate a problem involving a defined area. Students create and write stories about situations in which their parents have given them an area of the backyard (for example, 12, 18, or 32 square feet) for a project. There are many questions the students need to answer through their explorations:

1. What will your area's purpose be (for example, animal pen, swimming pool, garden, clubhouse)?

2. How many different rectangular areas are there for that defined area?

3. What are the dimensions of each rectangular array? The perimeter of each?

4. Which rectangular array best suits the purpose?

This project meets the needs of my diverse student population, in that each student can choose an idea that interests him or her (animals, swimming, gardening, building, and so on). Also, all students can be successful because the defined areas can be adjusted for the divergent learning levels (smaller areas for those who struggle with math and greater areas for those who are more capable of grasping the concepts).

After formulating a problem and writing a story about it, the students begin exploring, inquiring, and problem solving. They use color tiles to build each possible rectangular array and then record each on grid paper. After finding all possible configurations, the students label the dimensions and calculate the perimeters, understanding that although the area never changes, the perimeters usually do.

The Communication National Standard states that students will "organize . . . their mathematical thinking through communication;

communicate their mathematical thinking coherently and clearly to peers, teachers, and others." My students accomplish this goal by communicating their story problems and resultant solutions through a PowerPoint presentation in which they create slides to share their stories, show all the possible arrays (created using the Draw application in Microsoft Word), show and explain the best configuration for their project, import digital pictures, scan in samples of their hand-drawn arrays, and, most of all, reflect on the learning that has taken place.

Having students write about what they have just learned and put that knowledge in their own words helps me to diagnose misconceptions and problems the students are having before we move on to other activities or even a new unit. I also feel that self-reflection extends and deepens their understanding of the concepts presented. It is important that those students who are more capable extend their knowledge by posing a new question, such as, "What areas could I create if my parents gave me fencing for a perimeter of _____ feet?" This media presentation serves also as a part of the assessment of the knowledge garnered through this unit. These presentations are shown to family and friends at Family Math Night in January or at student-led conferences in March.

The second major project for this unit is one in which students learn that measurements in the real world are not always exact. This project is called "Make Room for Measurement," as several measurement concepts are included: area, perimeter, money, and time. The students find the areas and perimeters of the walls, floor, and ceiling of a "room" by measuring all sides of a box brought from home. They use estimation skills, since the lengths and widths are seldom exact. As the students make the measurements, calculate the costs, and estimate the time it will take, they record their findings in journal entries created in MS Word.

They explain their problem-solving process and the results. When all the preliminary work is complete, the students are allowed to create wallpaper for the walls, carpet for the floor, and border for the perimeter of the ceiling. The rules are that the designs need to fill the paper and have either line or rotational symmetry. They can create brick walls for the outside of the box, as well as doors and windows. All students experience success at their own levels of understanding. I enrich for those more capable by having them find the volume of their rooms as well.

This measurement unit is extensive and generally takes six to eight weeks to complete, but the benefits are numerous. The activities involve the students in number sense concepts of multiplication, division, and fractions, as well as probability and graphing, in addition to the measurement concepts and problem solving. Therefore, I believe that the unit is well worth the time spent. A sixth-grade teacher shared with me a few years ago that when she introduced area and perimeter to her class, several students stated that they knew that stuff already, because they'd made rooms in fourth grade. I call that successfully engaging students so that they retain learning!

Helpful Tip

- Engaging students is not an easy task. In my 25-plus years of teaching, I have discovered that it becomes possible when you love what you are doing and when that love spills over into creating activities that make mathematics relate to real life and, therefore, meaningful for students.

CHAPTER 16

Letting Everyone Shine

Carol Ann Amos

Plainfield, Vermont

R ecently, during a fluctuation in student population and with a
problem year with our school's budget, the two fourth-grade teachers at my school were faced with larger than usual classes. As mathematics coordinator, I volunteered to assist them by taking a portion of the
students during math time and having them in a class of my own. Students
were drawn from both classrooms, and I set up a makeshift classroom in
the corner of the elementary music room. The majority of my students
had unique learning needs. None of them was near the top of the class,
yet they were a wonderful group.

After a few weeks of being together and getting to know them,
I realized that these students had never had a chance to be the "stars"
during previous class times. Most of them were struggling, and their
feelings toward math and their belief in their abilities in this area were
less than ideal. Knowing that feeling confident in something and being
able to demonstrate your confidence by sharing your knowledge with
others is important to all learners, I decided to find a way for my
students to gain this confidence.

I developed an idea to create "experts" to help when we had an activity that was new and hands-on. The day before the activity, I would have lunch with a couple of my students. During this lunchtime, I would hold a mini-lesson on some of the activities we would be engaged in during the next day's exploration time. I would work with the students until they were ready to be my "expert" helper teachers. The next day, as we started the activity, my helper teachers would identify themselves as willing and able to jump in and help anyone as needed. They took their roles very seriously. They were wonderful at it, plus they genuinely demonstrated that they were the "experts."

I believe my idea was a success, but I didn't realize in how many ways it would be successful. Not only did the students gain confidence, but I gained a couple more teachers in my room. It was wonderful to be able to guide a student who needed help to one of their classmates, knowing that they would get the help they needed while I worked with other students. I didn't anticipate how seriously the students would take their roles as teachers.

Often I would overhear my helper teachers ask leading questions to another student; they would never just take over and do the work for the students they were instructing. I couldn't help but smile when I would hear one of my helper teachers say, "Good job, buddy!" or "You got it! Way to go!" to one of their "students." I learned a lot from my helper teachers. Most of all, I realized that we are losing a great opportunity when we don't provide a chance for all students to shine.

CHAPTER 17

From Angst to Aptitude

Math Is More Than a Four-Letter Word

John P. Pieper

Oshkosh, Wisconsin

So exactly when do students learn to dislike math? It seems as if somewhere along the line as they "learn" the skills of carrying, borrowing, decimals, and division, many students acquire a negative attitude toward math. By the time they get to my fifth-grade class, a large percentage of the students literally hate math, while only a small percentage like math. Adding to the problem, parents are often as frustrated as the students. All things being equal, the challenges are multiplied by the factors of high-stakes testing, larger classes, and fewer resources. How are we as teachers supposed to measure up to the expectations?

Task 1: How many math terms can you find in the above paragraph? Count the number of words and sentences, and then determine the average number of words in each sentence. Finally, measure the dimensions of the paragraph and calculate the perimeter and area. Work with a partner and be ready to give your answers in ten minutes.

From greater-than and less-than alligators to rubber band rubrics, a creative teacher can help reduce the math anxiety that many students face. From the very first math lesson each year, one of my main goals is to do whatever it takes to make sure all the students gain the confidence they need to be successful in math. A carpenter cannot build a house with only a hammer and a screwdriver. Likewise, all too often children are moved on to the next grade without possessing all the tools they need to build their math skills.

Fewer than half of my 22 students had true mastery of their multiplication facts at the start of the school year. Their introduction to math with me began with a story:

When I was in high school, we had a really good football team. In fact, we were going to be the conference champions if we could win the last game of the season. But there was one problem. The star player on the team was failing math. If he couldn't get a passing grade by the day of the big game, he couldn't play.

The coach went to the math teacher and begged him to give the star player a break. At first, the math teacher said no, but then he made a deal with the coach. If the star player could pass a simple facts test, then the star player could play in the big game.

All week the coach worked with the star player. They practiced and practiced the multiplication facts. By Friday, the day of the test, the coach and his player were ready. The star player confidently walked into the classroom, sat down, and was handed the test by the stern-looking math teacher. The star player looked at the test and panicked. He was staring at the hardest of the facts, the nines. Even worse, the math teacher said he had only five minutes in which to complete the test.

The math teacher left and the star player started working on the test.

$0 \times 9 =$ _____ $1 \times 9 =$ _____ $2 \times 9 =$ _____ $3 \times 9 =$ _____ $4 \times 9 =$ _____

$5 \times 9 =$ _____ $6 \times 9 =$ _____ $7 \times 9 =$ _____ $8 \times 9 =$ _____ $9 \times 9 =$ _____

(Fill in the answers as you tell the story.)

He remembered that any number times zero is zero. He also remembered that any number times one is the number. He looked at the other problems and the pressure got to him. His mind went blank. Two minutes passed and nothing. Three minutes passed, and the star player was getting very worried. Four minutes passed, and he just gave up. To see how badly he had failed, he decided to see how many problems he had wrong. So he counted down the column of problems, filling in the numbers as he went. "One, two, three, four, five, six, seven, eight. Eight wrong! That can't be right." So he counted up from the bottom. "One, two, three, four, five, six, seven, eight." The math teacher walked in, looked at the paper, and wrote a big red A on the test. The star player got to play in the big game, and we won the championship.

The students are always amazed and amused when they hear this story. They often want to know if there are other math tricks that work as well as this one. Their questions lead to the first of many discussions that will encourage them to develop more positive attitudes toward math. One of the key components to helping the students find success in math is to demand that they master their basic addition, subtraction, multiplication, and division facts.

"Drill and kill" practices are not in vogue right now, but educationally, there are some things that students just have to memorize. Teachers and parents from one grade level to the next have to be diligent in making sure each child acquires these fundamental skills. We strive for reading fluency. Why should we settle for anything less when we are teaching the basic facts? Take the time to do it right the first time.

This doesn't necessarily mean that the students need to do page after page of written practice. There are the tried-and-true methods such as flash cards, oral practice, and quizzes. Teachers can tap into resources including peer tutors, students as mentors for younger students, grandparent volunteers, and the multitude of programs available on computers. One technique that can be used to sharpen their skills is the use of Samurai Semaphore math.

Through a series of hand signals, the students must mentally solve math problems. A vertical hand with the pinkie facing the students is used as the plus symbol. A horizontal hand is the sign for subtraction. A closed fist is multiplication, and two hands forming an X are used for division. To make an equals sign, make a V with two fingers and turn it horizontally. So if I hold up three fingers, a closed fist, five fingers, a horizontal hand, three fingers, and an equals sign, the answer is 12.

Samurai Semaphore is a great way to warm up a math class. It can be used to fill in that minute or two your class has while waiting for an assembly to start. The students can use it to challenge each other during indoor recesses. Have the students teach it to their parents and siblings. But be prepared to defend it. One teacher wanted to know why I was teaching the kids karate.

It is very important for the teacher to critically analyze his or her role as a math teacher. Are you locked into the lessons as they are presented in the book, or are you finding creative ways to make the math meaningful? Are you helping the students make connections between the math they do and the applications of math in the real world? How are you addressing the needs of each child? Raise your expectations.

Helpful Tips

- Strive for mastery of the basic facts. They are the foundations from which student success in math is built.
- Make it fun. Learn the tricks and stories that will help reduce math anxiety.
- Make it meaningful. Math should be a part of their lives and not just a class.
- Include the parents. If math is important at home, it will be easier to teach at school.
- Shortages of time and money can be overcome with creative applications.
- Feel free to contact me.

CHAPTER 18

Lesson Study

A "Win-Win" Professional Practice

Debra Rose Howell

Granite Falls, Washington

> *Personally, the most beneficial part of lesson study was the camaraderie it built within our staff. We began with a group of teachers who were in no way a cohesive team. Our teachers are more comfortable with each other and respect each other's abilities. Student learning benefits as a result.*
>
> —Andrea Peterson, Music Specialist

Four years ago, our elementary staff was once again looking at state testing scores that were well below acceptable standards. Little growth had been shown in the areas of reading and mathematics on the state tests. I am a veteran multiage teacher—part of a four-member team that provides instruction to students in Grades 4 through 6. My team, in collaboration with fifth-grade teachers in our school, decided that we needed to make major changes in how we were preparing students for state tests.

As a National Board Certified Teacher, I have taken opportunities to meet with fellow certified teachers across the country. I attended a presentation by Tom White, a fellow NBCT, about Japanese lesson study and I decided to research it more. Upon doing so, I felt strongly that this was *just* what our staff might be able to easily incorporate and make significant changes for ourselves as educators and for our students. One problem: This particular group of teachers hadn't worked very cohesively in the past. Would lesson study work for us?

What Is Lesson Study?

Lesson study involves a team of educators who plan and implement a meaningful learning activity for their students. It is modeled after the Japanese form of lesson study, where it is their primary form of professional development. In the United States, teaching is extremely isolated. We often find little time as educators to actually talk professionally about lesson planning. When our experienced teachers retire, their best practices often retire with them. Haven't you attended workshops where you told yourself, "I know I could have done a better job presenting that material"? We need to utilize the expertise and resources we have in our own buildings on staff. Lesson study is an easy and cost-effective way to do just that!

With lesson study, the focus is on the lesson, *not* the teaching. Together a small team of teachers look closely at a lesson and tweak it until they get it down to where it works best for students. Lesson study is student centered and student driven.

How Does This Work?

The five steps of lesson study are:

1. The Whole Team Sets a Goal

- Long range, overarching
- "We want our students to understand . . ."

2. A Curricular Area Is Selected

- Examine data, such as state- or district-level test results
- Choose specific area to be focused upon

3. The Smaller Groups Plan the Lesson

- Everything is discussed
- Divergent ideas are debated
- The lesson is chosen or designed

4. One Team Member Teaches the Lesson

- The others watch and take notes
- Emphasis is on student learning

5. The Team Analyzes and Reflects

- Immediately after the lesson, identify what needs to be changed in the lesson
- Focus is on student learning
- The next team member reteaches the lesson
- Revised lesson is reviewed

How Do We Organize?

When we first started looking at the lesson study approach, I spoke with my principal and shared with him research about its use in Japan. I made copies of these articles and I distributed them to all of our fifth-grade staff, support staff, administrators, and paraprofessionals. I then held a meeting to discuss the possibilities of applying for a grant (to help fund the release time for staff) and to see what interest they might have as a staff. To my delight, *every* fifth-grade teacher and support staff member attended the meeting!

After reading the research and discussing it further as a group, we decided the timing was perfect for making essential changes to our program. There is an incredible amount of pressure on teachers and administrators to prepare students for the state tests. In our schools, a hands-on math curriculum had also been added so our teachers were overwhelmed. Finding enough time to read up and plan proper lessons was daunting.

The participants discussed how we would allocate the available time to attain our goals. We felt that choosing one math strand for each trimester would be most effective. This would become our focus for our first year of lesson study groups. Not only was the group of educators committed and enthusiastic about lesson study groups, but the administration, including the superintendent and school board, also watched to see what successes we might find.

Our focus for this first year was:

We will use Japanese lesson study techniques to better enable ourselves, as educators, to move from "teaching as telling" to "teaching for understanding." We will develop instruction that supports students' academic abilities, individuality, and needs.

From here we developed our goals.

Our Lesson Study Goals

1. Focus on the specific areas where our current fifth-grade students were below grade level on testing. Plan carefully the specific goals of the lesson. Assess the previous year's scores.

2. Collaborate with our fifth-grade teachers, specialists, paraprofessionals, and administrators.

3. Create an environment for reflection. Lesson planning will be done cooperatively where criticism is generally shared.

4. Build more time for planning, observing, discussing, and refining actual classroom lessons as a team of educators.

5. See measurable, across-the-board improvement on the spring fifth-grade state testing in mathematics.

⬚ What Happens?

We had four total teams of four or five teachers presenting weekly lessons, for a total of 19 educators participating this first year. Each team had a slightly different lesson they were working on. These four to five educators then met once a week to present a lesson, come back and meet to dissect the lesson, look at student work, and tweak the lesson for the next teacher to present the following week.

Each team held the first meeting to plan the math activity they wanted to use the following week. Everything from gathering supplies to photocopying to discussing the lesson plan was completed during this initial meeting. One teacher was chosen to present the team's lesson the following week. This was then followed up by a meeting after school. Student work was brought to the meetings so that educators could see firsthand the assignment the students had done. In addition, the team of observers brought the notes that they took while watching their lessons being presented to a classroom of students. Comments about students interacting and general comments on how the lesson worked with the students were taken. Then changes—no matter how small or how big—were made to the lesson as a team. The same lesson was repeated in the next teacher's room *with* the modifications made by the group. Throughout the modifications to the lessons, we always felt that it was *"our lesson,"* not just that of the teacher who was presenting. These team meetings can be done after school or with half-day substitutes. Both work well, but obviously teachers can be more effective if they have the half-day substitute time available.

At the conclusion of the first round of lesson study, all the small groups of four to five educators came together as one larger lesson study group. This built camaraderie with the larger staff throughout our lesson study process. Each small group presented the changes and "ah-has!" they had experienced while working together on their particular lesson. Normally the group leader shares student examples as well as lesson samples showing the specific changes that took place and how they impacted student learning. These meetings normally lasted for two to three hours while each group presented their findings to the larger group. Powerful professional discussions occur when these smaller groups share.

Lesson study teams show a PowerPoint presentation, overhead transparencies, or even videotapes from their classroom presentations to illustrate their discoveries. Teachers quickly broke down the walls around them and spoke freely about what worked and what didn't work. At the conclusion of each round, the larger group then established a new focus for the upcoming round. A new round of lesson study started a month or so later with a new mixture of group members and new group leaders. In addition, each group had a different curriculum specialist to work with. The specialists provided invaluable feedback, as they had not only experience with all the children in the school but also in different subject areas, such as music and physical education. Lesson study practice has also provided excellent teaching modeling for our paraprofessionals to see in action. The team-building aspect that started from the smaller groups quickly transferred over into the larger group setting. This then extended throughout the building.

Is It Worth It?

I gave the staff a survey to complete at the end of each year. These are some of the thoughts about what the staff members felt that students—and they themselves—had gained from this lesson study.

How Did Staff Feel That Students *Most Benefit From Lesson Study?*

- ". . . they benefited because I was able to observe seasoned teachers and put into practice what I observed."
- "They were exposed to lessons they might not have gotten if we hadn't planned together."
- ". . . exposure to varied instructional strategies through teacher collaboration . . . many styles of lessons implementation were discussed. A higher level of hands-on activities took place during the lessons."
- "I think the focus on one skill was the most powerful component for student learning. This is supported by the fact that state testing scores were significantly higher in this area. The use of *consistent* vocabulary used by teachers helped the students understand what was being asked of them."

How Did Staff Feel That They Most Benefit From Lesson Study?

- ". . . teamwork with colleagues thinking about lessons from different angles and the feedback that it creates . . ."
- "The camaraderie that it built in the staff with an uncohesive team . . ."
- "I was impressed with the positive comments from other staff and parents who were not participating . . . they said they hadn't heard such positive professional discussions ever!"
- "My feelings toward teaching math have really come together . . . I am much more confident in myself as a math teacher."
- "I love time to collaborate! I do my best thinking when I discuss. Also, being accountable to a team is motivating."

Overall we were *thrilled* with our first year of Japanese lesson study, Monte Cristo style! From our team discussions we all felt that we accomplished all of our initial goals. Our emphasis was always on *how this is impacting student learning.* This helped us to stay focused in our discussions, and as a result, staff and students benefited. We as a staff grew in our professionalism, camaraderie, renewed enthusiasm, and passion for teaching. Our state test score improved by an estimated 6 percent in the specific area of math that we focused on. This was the first time we had seen growth in this area! As a bonus, word was getting out to the rest of the staff about how nonthreatening and successful lesson study had been. Suddenly more people were interested in joining lesson study.

During our second year of lesson study, we again felt successful in reaching our goals. This year we moved to include the fourth-grade staff. The major change in the second year was moving from meeting after school to half-day release time. Everyone found this to be an ideal time to meet. Staff continued growth in our professionalism, and we were seeing a direct impact in our classrooms with student learning. Once again we were seeing a rise in student achievement as measured on the state assessments.

We recently completed our third year of lesson study, expanding to include every grade level, specialists, and staff from other buildings as observers. Nearly the entire staff participated! During this year, our focus was on *writing skills in conjunction with expository reading comprehension.* In addition to our weekly meetings for small teams and our larger group meeting at the end of each cycle, we added research discussion time.

Small-team leaders assigned a research article (dealing with reading in the intermediate years) that was to be read by the team, and a portion of the half-day release was for conversation regarding the research. This added another level of professional development to our lesson study groups. Our district reading specialist joined us. She gave insight and expertise to the small and larger group meetings. For example, she showed us how to take our nonfiction text used in science and write stem questions that were modeled from the style of questions the children would experience on the state test. Students were taught to pull examples directly from the given text and not to paraphrase their responses. We soon realized that the students simply needed to be given guidance and practice at doing this. They caught on very quickly.

Our 2005 state assessment scores in reading increased 14 percent from the previous year! This increase is due greatly to our focus in the lesson study groups on reading throughout that school year. This further reinforces our efforts in lesson study, as no changes in reading curriculum were made. We used the research and information gained from our discussions and transferred that knowledge beyond the lesson study rounds into other aspects of our curriculum. For example, we were better able to take science and social studies topics and incorporate the stem questioning techniques that we learned and refined during lesson study.

Now as we begin our fourth year of incorporating our own form of Japanese lesson study across our elementary school, I feel confident that this form of professional development is directly impacting student learning. In addition, it is helping to build a professional camaraderie that prepares teachers for the classroom realities of challenging educational mandates and high expectations on state testing. We can more effectively elicit the expertise of teacher resources in our own buildings to better serve our students. Teachers are becoming more highly qualified and more confident in their own teaching. In the end, both students and staff reap the benefits in this "win-win" form of professional development.

Helpful Tips

- The lesson study process needs to start with a trusted experienced staff member, *not* with the administrator.
- Keep it a voluntary form of staff professional development. Start slowly.
- Make sure there is a leader in each group who will keep the smaller groups focused and on task. This also helps to build more teacher leaders among your staff.

Index

**CORWIN
PRESS**

The Corwin Press logo—a raven striding across an open book—represents the union of courage and learning. Corwin Press is committed to improving education for all learners by publishing books and other professional development resources for those serving the field of PreK–12 education. By providing practical, hands-on materials, Corwin Press continues to carry out the promise of its motto: **"Helping Educators Do Their Work Better."**